THE URBANA FREE LIBRARY
3 1230 00943 3521

W9-AXG-737

ORCA FOOTPRINTS

Better Together

CREATING COMMUNITY IN AN UNCERTAIN WORLD

NIKKI TATE

ORCA BOOK PUBLISHERS

Library and Archives Canada Cataloguing in Publication

Tate, Nikki, 1962-, author
Better together : creating community in an uncertain world / Nikki Tate.
(Orca footprints)

Includes bibliographical references and index.
Issued in print and electronic formats.
ISBN 978-1-4598-1300-7 (hardcover).—ISBN 978-1-4598-1301-4 (pdf).—
ISBN 978-1-4598-1302-1 (epub)

1. Communities—Juvenile literature. 2. Fellowship—Juvenile literature. 3. Social groups—Juvenile literature. 4. Social participation—Juvenile literature. I. Title. II. Series: Orca footprints

HM756.T38 2018 j307 C2017-904572-5
C2017-904573-3

First published in the United States, 2018
Library of Congress Control Number: 2017949703

Summary: Part of the nonfiction Footprints series for middle readers, illustrated with many color photographs. Explore the different types of communities people create to meet their need for companionship.

Orca Book Publishers is dedicated to preserving the environment and has printed this book on Forest Stewardship Council® certified paper.

Orca Book Publishers gratefully acknowledges the support for its publishing programs provided by the following agencies: the Government of Canada through the Canada Book Fund and the Canada Council for the Arts, and the Province of British Columbia through the BC Arts Council and the Book Publishing Tax Credit.

Cover images by Stocksy.com, Getty Images
Back cover images (top left to right): Tony Sprackett, Shutterstock.com, Dreamstime.com (bottom left to right): iStock.com, Shutterstock.com, iStock.com

Edited by Sarah N. Harvey
Design and production by Teresa Bubela and Jenn Playford

ORCA BOOK PUBLISHERS
www.orcabook.com

Printed and bound in Canada.

21 20 19 18 • 4 3 2 1

During the seventh annual Hands Across the Sand event in 2017, thousands of people gathered in Australia, Egypt, Belize and New Zealand to say NO to fossil fuels and YES to clean energy. YANA MAVLYUTOVA/SHUTTERSTOCK.COM

For the many writers, editors, publishers and readers in my wonderful community of word-lovers.

Contents

CHAPTER THREE: GO BIG!

CHAPTER FOUR: AROUND THE GLOBE

Introduction

Food, water, shelter and a safe, clean environment are all essential if humans are going to thrive. Just as important, though, is a sense of *community*. It's nearly impossible to meet the basic human need for love, acceptance, safety and security if you live in total *isolation*. Fortunately, we have many opportunities to bond with others. Working together, we can create healthy, productive, safe communities where people look after each other.

Visiting family can mean traveling halfway around the world to spend time together. Here I am sharing special time with family in Paris. OLGA LITMANOVA FOR FLYTOGRAPHER

Too often we look at someone and see all the ways we are different. *Better Together* looks at the many ways we are the same no matter where we live. People everywhere come together to build things, teach and entertain each other and provide everything from better health care and good food to security and education.

Sometimes, when we forget that people are more similar than different, we feel afraid. Sadly, fear and anger can make us say and do things we regret. Focusing on differences can tear families and communities apart.

In *Better Together* we'll explore how people gather in groups of all kinds to fulfill basic human needs. From the smallest units of parents, siblings and best friends, to global organizations that try to build on a foundation of common human experience to meet their goals, people working together are a powerful force for change.

We all need to love and be loved, to look after others and to feel looked after. DGLIMAGES/ISTOCK.COM

Maslow's Hierarchy of Needs

SELF-ACTUALIZATION	1
SELF-ESTEEM	2
LOVE AND BELONGING	3
SAFETY AND SECURITY	4
PHYSIOLOGICAL NEEDS	5

In 1943 the American psychologist Abraham Maslow proposed a theory that described how people become psychologically healthy.

If all of their basic needs (3-5) are met, people can build their self-esteem, develop confidence, achieve their goals and concentrate on learning. For some, learning and development continue throughout their lives as they explore their creativity, develop a sense of right and wrong and polish their problem-solving and critical-thinking skills.

CHAPTER ONE

The First Community

A human baby would not survive without someone to provide food, shelter and affection.
GEORGE RUDY/SHUTTERSTOCK.COM

WELCOME TO THE WORLD

One of the most basic human bonds is between a mother and her child. The young of some species are pretty independent right from the start. For example, a foal (baby horse) can stand and run within hours of being born. Human babies are totally dependent on adults for several years. Though a mother, father and one or more children make up one type of family (sometimes called a *nuclear family*), many households are composed of other combinations of people. Ideally, the family unit makes sure that children are provided with everything needed to grow up and become healthy, happy members of society.

COMMUNITY FACT:
It's estimated that 255 babies are born each minute worldwide.

THE ESSENTIALS

In 1989, the United Nations International Children's Emergency Fund (UNICEF) established the Convention on the Rights of the Child. The UNICEF Convention described all the things a

This grandmother in the village of Mai Chau in Vietnam helps care for her grandchildren. BIDOUZE STÉPHANE/DREAMSTIME.COM

child needs to grow up and be healthy. For the first time, countries around the world agreed that children are individuals with rights to safe housing, a good education, access to health care, clean water and adequate food. The Convention also states that these rights should be extended to children no matter what their religion or *ethnicity*. Adopted children, *refugees*, children being raised by grandparents or other family members, or orphans being looked after by the government all deserve the same treatment. Children everywhere should be encouraged to grow and develop in a way that allows them to explore their own unique interests and talents.

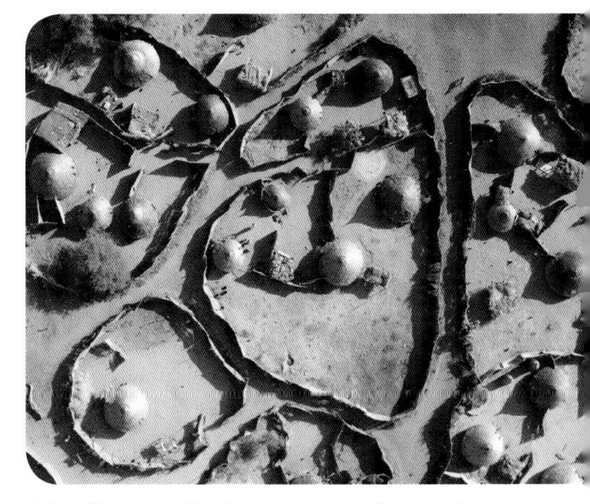

This village in Chad is made up of several family compounds. Each compound has numerous small houses for the different branches of a large family. Living so close together means the family can share responsibility for tasks like childcare or looking after an elderly relative. At the same time, the smaller, separate houses allow for some privacy. ECOIMAGESPHOTOS/DREAMSTIME.COM

SO MANY KINDS OF FAMILIES

In some households, two parents and one or more children live under the same roof. If parents no longer live together, children may divide their time between two homes. In many countries and cultures, it's not unusual for grandparents, uncles and aunts,

Love This!

WEEKEND IMAGES INC./ISTOCK.COM

I was lucky to have a warm extended family to help me raise my daughter. But not everyone is in the same position. CoAbode is an organization in the United States that matches single moms who would like to share housing with other single mothers. Pooling their resources means mothers can afford better housing for their families. Moms who team up and live together can also share responsibilities for cooking, shopping and other household duties. Children living in these shared homes have live-in companions.

cousins or other relatives to share a home with children and their parents. In some cases, a baby may be born to a family while a great-grandparent is still alive.

I CHOOSE YOU!

Sometimes a parent is unable to care for a baby and decides to give the child up for *adoption*. The child's adoptive family takes on the role of providing everything the child needs. In open adoptions, the *birth parents* stay in touch with the child and the adoptive family. In other cases, it's only after the child is an adult that it's possible for them to learn the identity of their birth parents.

There are many reasons why people decide to adopt a child. Sometimes the reasons are medical, sometimes it's because a *same-sex couple* wants a child, and some people want to share their lives with babies and children who have lost their birth families in a war or natural disaster.

BEST FRIENDS FOREVER

UNICEF recognizes just how important friends can be during a crisis. One of the reasons why it's so important to establish temporary schools in places like refugee camps is that the classroom environment also allows children to make friends. Having someone to talk to, particularly a friend who has gone through the same thing, can help a person cope with even the most stressful experiences.

Of course, you don't need to grow up in a war zone to appreciate the social connections made at school. My daughter, Dani, met one of her best friends, Alex, when they were both in second grade. Many years later, Alex was Dani's maid of honor at her wedding. I'm sure when Alex gets married, or when one of these young women starts a family of her own, both will share in the excitement.

Dani and Alex have been friends since they were seven years old.
NICHOLE TAYLOR PHOTOGRAPHY

FIRST FRIENDS

If a family has more than one child, siblings may be very close. A brother or sister could be someone's first real friend.

The first friends a child makes outside the family are sometimes introduced by parents. A child may discover new friends by attending play groups, daycare or preschool. As children get older, they have more opportunities to meet friends outside the family.

Some twins spend so much time together as children, they develop their own private language. This phenomenon is called cryptophasia. MURIEL LASURE/SHUTTERSTOCK.COM

TIME FOR SCHOOL

Schools are much more than places to learn to read or study math or science. Learning to get along with others is important too, and students can explore things they may not have access to at home—like art, drama, woodworking, cooking or dance. Sometimes, passions discovered at school develop into long-term career paths.

COMMUNITY FACT:
According to a *Washington Post* analysis of census data, the number of single-parent households has approximately doubled in the United States since 1960.

Students in this school in Tamil Nadu, India, meet regularly for lessons, but also to spend time with friends.
LEBLOND CATHERINE/DREAMSTIME.COM

I first discovered my love of writing in grade five when a teacher encouraged me to make up stories. When I learned that writing stories and books could be a profession, I was thrilled.

IT'S THE LAW!

In the 1970s, many people were concerned about world *overpopulation*: if too many babies were born each year, how could the world produce enough food to feed everyone?

In China in 1979, the Chinese government decided to restrict the number of children to one per family. The one-child policy was in place for more than thirty years. Though there were some exceptions (families in rural areas, for example, were allowed to have more than one child), the policy was effective in slowing China's population growth rate. However, some long-term effects are now causing a new set of problems. For example, with fewer young people entering the workforce, there are fewer workers to support older citizens.

COMMUNITY FACT:
According to the Guinness Book of World Records, the largest number of children born to one woman is sixty-nine. Valentina Vassilyev, the first wife of Feodor Vassilyev, lived in Russia in the 1700s, and over the course of 27 pregnancies she delivered sixteen pairs of twins, seven sets of triplets and four sets of quadruplets. She was one busy mom!

I Believe in Love

When my daughter was born, I lived with my parents and youngest brother. My daughter, Dani, knew her grandparents almost as well as she knew me. My parents and I shared parenting responsibilities, so it was almost like she had three parents rather than a single mother.

Though Dani calls my youngest brother "Uncle," in reality he was more like an older brother to her while she was growing up.
NIKKI TATE

In 2015, the government began to phase out the one-child policy. Families in China are now officially allowed to have two children, though many are choosing not to have larger families because raising children can be quite expensive.

A government may also get involved when a child's natural parents are unable to care for them properly. Sometimes a court or government agency decides to temporarily remove children from their homes and place them with foster families. *Foster parents* are people who provide short-term care for children who can't live with their parents for some reason. Whenever possible, parents (who may have trouble with substance abuse, be physically violent or be unable to care for their children for other reasons) are given treatment, counseling or other assistance until they are able to provide a safe, comfortable home for their kids.

In China, it's common to see families with a single child enjoying a meal together at a restaurant like this one in Beijing.

ANGELA OSTAFICHUK/SHUTTERSTOCK.COM

Let's Work Together

BARBERSHOP FILMS

Many classrooms look similar: a teacher stands at the front and students sit at desks studying a specific lesson. But some schools, like Windsor House in Vancouver, BC, let the children decide what and when they would like to learn. Different ages of students mix according to interests and abilities, and teachers provide support and encouragement rather than deciding what the day's lessons will include. Parents and older students share their knowledge and enthusiasm for a wide variety of subjects. Children help make decisions about how the school is run by participating in regular planning meetings, and their contributions and suggestions are taken very seriously. Play is not seen as a waste of time but as an important activity. Children are encouraged to play throughout the day and not just during breaks from studying. If you could choose how to spend your day at school, what would you do?

CHAPTER TWO

In the 'Hood

MEET YOUR NEIGHBORS

Most people in the world live in populated areas. The people who live closest to you are your neighbors, and groups of nearby residents form a neighborhood. If you live in a rural community, the closest neighbor may be several kilometers down the road. If you live in the heart of a big city, you may share an apartment building with hundreds of other families.

One of the largest apartment buildings in the world is Le Lignon. Located in Switzerland, this building is about a kilometer (over half a mile) long and is home to almost 7,000 people. PORT(U*O)S/WIKIPEDIA.ORG

LIFESTYLE COMMUNITIES

The people who live close to you make up one type of community. Groups of people who move around a lot can still stay in touch and form a kind of portable neighborhood. People who live on their sailboats full time often move from place to place according to wind, weather and a desire to visit new places. When they drop their anchors or visit marinas, it's quite common to meet up with sailors they've spent time with at other locations. Sometimes cruisers travel in groups,

These boys in Cuba play in the street, proving that getting to know people in your neighborhood is one way to make sure you always have someone to play with. NIKADA/ISTOCK.COM

Children gather at their local 4-H club to learn about taking care of their pigs.
CREATISTA/SHUTTERSTOCK.COM

COMMUNITY FACT:
A group of people of a similar age is called an *age cohort*.

keeping in contact during ocean crossings. Boats may share information about weather conditions or provide assistance if something breaks. On land, people who live in their motor homes, converted school buses or other movable homes meet up in places like campgrounds and parks and create a similar kind of portable community.

Communities also form around activities. Climbers, for example, regularly run into friends while visiting mountains far from home. Groups of climbers often team up, sharing experience and equipment as they tackle climbs that may range from single-day outings on sport crags to major expeditions that might last weeks or months.

Some older people prefer to travel to places where children and families are discouraged. The Villages is a huge retirement community in Florida where more than 100,000 people over the age of 55 choose to live. Many of the residents travel around using golf carts. It's estimated there are about 50,000 golf carts in the community, many of which have been painted with bright colors and fancy designs or made to look like antique cars.

People may also gather because they share an interest in music, art, food or a particular sport. The 28 square kilometers (7,000 acres) of Casa de Campo in the Dominican Republic includes a fancy golf course surrounded by villas where golf-loving residents live. What you might not expect to find in the Caribbean, though, is the replica of a sixteenth-century Mediterranean village. Altos de Chavón is accurate in every detail right down to its cobblestone streets, ancient-looking buildings and an amphitheater. Artist studios, shops, cafes, a marina and spa keep golfers busy when they aren't playing their favorite game.

ONLINE COMMUNITIES

Whether you love salsa dancing, ice hockey, equestrian vaulting or collecting buttons, chances are there are many other people who also enjoy your passion. There may be a group in your town that meets to take part in a particular activity, but if not, online communities can be a good way for people to share information about a hobby.

Though most of the people you are likely to meet online to discuss a particular interest are perfectly nice, be smart when you are online. Never give out your personal information (your address, full name, phone number) and don't agree to meet up with someone you only know online. Let an adult know if you feel uncomfortable about something you come across online. Check with your parents before posting photos of yourself or others online, and let someone know right away if you receive messages that are mean or make you feel bad in any way.

Kids around the world with a shared interest can connect with each other online.
LISA F. YOUNG/DREAMSTIME.COM

Let's Work Together

IAN ALLENDEN /DREAMSTIME.COM

In many places around the world it is common for people of different generations to live together. In other places, like North America, Australia and some countries in Europe, it's just as likely that seniors either live alone, far from their families, or in nursing homes with other elderly people. Studies have shown that seniors who interact with people of different ages are happier and healthier.

At the Humanitas nursing home in the Netherlands, six college students live rent-free in the nursing home in exchange for providing thirty hours per month of being "good neighbors." Chatting and hanging out with their much older friends turns out to have benefits for both groups of residents. The older residents focus less on sickness and dying and enjoy having conversations about school, parties and dating with their youthful neighbors. The students not only find a solution to the extreme shortage of student housing, but they also learn some valuable lessons about being happy and enjoying life. Though the program may have started out with purely practical goals, the end result is that all the residents, young and old, have discovered a sense of family, friendship and fun in their unusual living arrangement.

This little girl has no fear of the chameleon. Connecting with other reptile lovers is a way for her to learn about the best way to care for her unusual pet.
WALDRU /DREAMSTIME.COM

If your passion is somewhat unusual, like spiders, it may be hard to learn more about the best way to collect, preserve and organize your specimens without using the Internet. Online communities provide lots of information, and they can also be a great way to connect with spider collectors from around the world. Sometimes online communities also have a real-world aspect. Members of the American Tarantula Society receive a magazine all about spiders, have access to online discussions, can download all sorts of information about tarantulas, scorpions and other spiders, and can even attend the organization's annual convention. You may be the only person in your neighborhood who likes the idea of cuddling up with a tarantula, but you are not alone!

WORKING TOGETHER

Employees may spend many years together at their place of work. In North America, it's common for people to work forty hours each week with only two weeks of vacation each year. If someone starts work at the age of twenty and retires at age sixty-five, that person could spend more than 90,000 hours at work. Though it's not unusual for people to change careers several times (and to have various jobs within each career), that still means workers spend many hours each day with the same group of people.

Healthy workplaces encourage employees to get to know each other personally and provide opportunities to socialize on company time. Some companies offer fun outings like bowling or field trips, and others may provide on-site yoga, dance classes or art lessons. Keeping employees happy and feeling part of a group means workers stay with a company longer.

The offices of Infosys include a bowling alley and swimming pool. Creating places for employees to hang out and have fun can be a great way to encourage friendships at work.
INDIANHILBILLY/WIKIPEDIA.ORG

The Google offices in California have a reputation for being a fun place to work. VITALIY POZDEEV/DREAMSTIME.COM

I Believe in Love

When I was a child, my family moved around a lot. By tenth grade I was attending my tenth school. Even though I can be quite shy, as a child I had to learn how to talk to new people and make friends so that settling into a new school would be a little easier. Much later in life I took up climbing and sailing as serious hobbies. The skills I learned as a child have been useful when I meet people who sail or climb. Though these communities are both based on the shared love of an activity rather than moving into a new neighborhood, making new friends still works the same way it did when I was much younger. If you find it hard to connect with new people, try a big smile and ask a question. Before you know it, you will be chatting away and learning all kinds of things about your new friends.

Each day during this family sailing trip in the Caribbean, we anchored our sailboat and then took the dinghy to the nearest island. Once ashore we met new people from all over the world. NIKKI TATE

Love This!

ANDREW DAVIDSON/WIKIPEDIA.ORG

The Simon Community in London, England, has been helping the homeless community since 1963. Homeless people and volunteers work together to provide food, hot drinks and various services to those living in the streets of the city. Mobile street cafes set up by Simon Community volunteers are places where people can meet friends, have a snack and play chess without worrying about being asked to leave. Some volunteers also live full-time in communal houses with some of those who have been living rough. Everyone in the house shares household responsibilities, eats meals together and actively works toward creating "an atmosphere of love and acceptance."

CHOOSE YOUR FRIENDS CAREFULLY

Gang membership is often associated with violence, drug use and criminal activity. For some gang members, the desire to belong to a group where they feel powerful and needed is just too hard to resist. The Los Angeles Police Department (LAPD) lists a number of reasons why young people join gangs. These include a need for protection if they live in an area with lots of gang activity or a desire to get involved in criminal activity.

The LAPD also notes that for many gang members, friendship and companionship may be lacking at home, and the gang provides a kind of extended family. Sadly, the price for membership in a gang family is often very high. Turf wars between gangs can lead to serious injury or death. Continued membership may require the gang member to get more and more deeply involved in criminal activities, which, in turn, can lead to decades of jail time.

PLACES WE DON'T WANT TO BE

Prison

Sometimes people live together without actually making the decision to do so. A prison is an example of a place where people who don't want to be there may spend time (often a very long time) together. As in any community, members have responsibilities (prisoners may take classes, perform specific jobs or tasks, or participate in programs) and there are rules that must be followed.

Though being in prison is tough for anyone, incarcerated men and women may form strong bonds. Friendships can last long after prisoners have been released.

A woman may have to go to jail while she is pregnant. Recognizing the importance of the bond that forms early between a mother and her new baby, some prisons provide a nursery for new mothers. The oldest prison nursery in the United States is in New York State and has been operating since 1901. After the first year, babies are no longer allowed to stay with their mothers. The prison provides a special visiting room and a daily visiting program for older children, as well as programs that help train the mothers so they will have a better chance of finding jobs after they have been released.

Some prisons partner with organizations that train service dogs for veterans who have suffered injuries while serving in the military. Prisoners are taught how to care for and train dogs that will later help veterans who suffer from a range of physical and emotional injuries. The prisoners learn valuable job skills and the dogs provide support for military personnel who need assistance.

The Mexican singer Gloria Trevi speaks to a group of women inmates at the same prison in which she served time years ago.

PHOTOGENIAMEXICO/DREAMSTIME.COM

Leper Colonies

Leprosy (also called Hansen's disease) is caused by a type of bacteria. The symptoms of the disease include lumps, bumps or sores on the skin that don't go away. Nerve damage may be painful or lead to numbness. Leprosy patients may live with the disease for many years. Before the discovery of antibiotics, healthy people were afraid of catching this contagious disease. Leper colonies provided places for affected people to live out their lives. Some were located in isolated places to prevent contact with healthy people. Kalawao, on the island of Molokai in Hawaii, was a leper colony from 1866 until the early 1900s. During the years of operation, thousands of people were quarantined there.

D'Arcy Island, off British Columbia's west coast, was used to isolate Chinese Canadians who suffered from leprosy. Four times a year a boat dropped supplies on the beach, but otherwise the residents of D'Arcy Island were left to fend for themselves. Between the early 1890s and 1924, forty-nine unfortunate Chinese leprosy sufferers were sent to this sad community. In this case, *racism* and *discrimination*

The Greek island of Kalydon was one of the last leper colonies in Europe. It operated between 1903 and 1957.

MALAMANT/WIKIPEDIA.ORG

Love This!

ROMRODPHOTO/SHUTTERSTOCK.COM

At the Kipling Acres Long-term Care Home in Toronto, Ontario, seniors enjoy sharing their building with children who attend the daycare center downstairs. Several times a week the two groups get together to dance, cook, do crafts and share other activities. The seniors love the interaction with their exuberant young friends. The children learn to get along with much older people who may be in wheelchairs or use canes or walkers and who may not behave the same way as family members at home.

(Chinese immigrants were not liked in Canada at the time) combined with fear and misunderstanding of the disease led local politicians to treat Chinese leprosy patients particularly poorly.

Today, Hansen's disease is treated with antibiotics. Even though it is considered curable, in some places old ideas are slow to change and patients are still *ostracized*. Groups like the World Health Organization are working hard to educate people everywhere, starting by calling the illness Hansen's disease rather than leprosy, a word with such a negative history.

HERE TODAY, GONE TOMORROW

The world's oldest city is believed to have been built in the area of the world known as Mesopotamia approximately 6,500 years ago. There is some debate over which city was actually the first, but Uruk (the site is being explored by archaeologists in modern-day Iraq) is believed to have first been settled in 4500 BCE. Byblos (a port city in the Mediterranean) is thought by many to be the oldest still-inhabited city. People have lived there for thousands of years.

At the other end of the scale are temporary cities that are built to house and support a large number of people for a very short period of time. Every four years, thousands of athletes gather to compete at the Olympic Games. They need to live, eat and train somewhere while they are far from home. Host nations spend millions of dollars building the equivalent of a small city for the athletes and their coaches. After the games are over, housing and sport facilities are often used by local community members.

Other temporary villages are built to support thousands of people who may gather for a short time to attend a music festival or sporting event. Even if people only come together for several days, they still need accommodation, food and somewhere to go to the bathroom. Large events also need security, first aid and, often, facilities for members of the media.

COMMUNITY FACT:

The largest athletes' village to date was built in Rio de Janeiro in 2016 when Brazil hosted the Summer Olympics. The dining hall was able to provide meals for 5,000 people at a time.

Members of Brazil's Olympic team celebrate at the Olympic Village in Rio de Janeiro in 2016.
A.RICARDO/SHUTTERSTOCK.COM

Refugee camps provide a place to stay for people fleeing their homes because of war, natural disaster or famine, or for economic or environmental reasons. Basic services like education, healthcare, security and sanitation are usually provided by governments or non-profit organizations. Refugee camps are meant to provide temporary shelter, but sometimes people wind up staying in them for years. Living accommodations are usually tents or simple shelters made of whatever local materials can be found. Recently the Swedish furniture chain IKEA came up with a much sturdier alternative. Packed in two cartons, IKEA's temporary shelters provide 17.5 square meters (188 square feet) of living space and include a solar panel on the roof. Four hours of light each night or the ability to charge a cell phone can make a huge difference in the quality of life of a camp resident. Other features, like a locking door and solid walls, improve privacy and security. The shelters are so much better than existing housing options in refugee camps, the design has won several prestigious awards and more than ten thousand have been erected in locations around the world.

Shelters like these could provide a more efficient and longer-term form of housing during an emergency. ©IKEA FOUNDATION/ÅSA SJÖSTRÖM

LET'S CREATE A VILLAGE!

Sometimes like-minded people decide to create a place to live together where they can explore shared ideas and lifestyles. Known as *intentional communities*, these planned communities are often formed by people who share spiritual, social or political ideas. Living and working closely together, members of an intentional community agree to certain rules and principles, which often revolve around ideas of cooperation, partnership and teamwork.

If the intentional community has a strong focus on environmental and economic sustainability, it may be known as an *ecovillage*.

Early Israeli kibbutzim *were planned cooperative communities based on farming.* EVERETT HISTORICAL/SHUTTERSTOCK.COM

Celebrations like this maypole dance at O.U.R. Ecovillage on Vancouver Island bring residents and visitors together to take part in traditions that have their origins hundreds of years ago. BRANDY GALLAGHER/O.U.R. ECOVILLAGE

In the United States in the 1960s and 1970s, many people found it hard to get jobs. Others had trouble fitting back into society after returning from fighting in Vietnam. Still others disagreed with keeping different races separate (*segregation*) and limiting opportunities for women (*misogyny*). Some people who wanted to fight these inequalities created *communes* with shared living spaces. Often these communes were located in agricultural areas, and members grew their own food.

In neighborhoods where people don't have yards, a community garden plot can be a space to grow vegetables, flowers and herbs as well as spend time with friends and neighbors. HERO IMAGES/GETTY.COM

COMMUNITY FACT: **According to the Global Ecovillage Network, there are more than 13,000 eco-settlements located on all six continents.**

CHAPTER THREE

Go Big!

Friends, family, neighbors and co-workers can all provide acceptance, friendship and support. But people are also drawn together in larger groups based on factors like shared religious ideas, race or ethnicity. Though these areas of common ground can bring people together, members of one group can sometimes disagree and even fight with members of another. This chapter will look at how these bonds and tensions can both bring us together and push us apart.

These children in Vienna, Austria, wear white robes to a service held at a Catholic church. In 2013, almost 65 percent of Austrians were Catholics.

RADIOKAFKA/SHUTTERSTOCK.COM

RELIGION

About 84 percent of the world's population practices at least one religion. Why is religion so important to people?

Despite differences in how various religions handle the details, most try to provide guidance in terms of teaching people moral values and showing them how to behave as part of a community. Religions try to answer complex questions about the meaning of life and what happens after we die. They also describe a particular set of beliefs relating to a person's spiritual life. Because religions have many members, it's natural that communities form wherever followers gather. Shared beliefs, activities, rituals and expectations for behavior all help bring a group of people together. In some religious or spiritual traditions, children have special classes where they learn a particular set of teachings. In other traditions, children and adults take part in ceremonies and worship sessions together.

In many religious traditions it's possible to spend time living with others who are very serious about learning all they can of a particular set of religious beliefs and practices. In several Christian and Buddhist traditions, a group of religious women (nuns) who live and study together are known as a *convent.* A group of religious men (monks) is called a *monastery.* The places where such religious studies take place are known as convents and monasteries.

COMMUNITY FACT:
It's estimated that there are about 4,200 religions and spiritual practices observed around the world.

Child monks playing outside the Tawang monastery in India. ISSAMYAL/DREAMSTIME.COM

COMMUNITY FACT: Jesse Jackson, an African American civil rights activist, popularized the term African American, believing it would put Americans with ancestors from Africa on the same footing as Irish Americans, Italian Americans or any other sort of American.

RACIAL AND ETHNIC IDENTITIES

Do you know where your grandparents were born? Your great-grandparents? Thinking about where we came from is one way that we develop a sense of who we are. Our racial and ethnic backgrounds help to create our identities but there is a lot of debate about what the words *race* and *ethnicity* actually mean.

According to a United Nations Educational, Scientific and Cultural Organization (UNESCO) statement in 1950, "race is not so much a biological phenomenon as a social myth." People living in different parts of the world have developed certain physical characteristics in response to environmental factors, but all humans belong to the same species. Race, when looked at from this perspective, is simply a way that people group themselves.

Though the underlying biology may be nearly identical, the perception of racial difference has been both a way of establishing bonds between people and a way to discriminate and *persecute* others based on superficial characteristics.

Ethnic groups are formed by those who share a *culture* that includes a particular language and set of customs and beliefs. A person may claim more than one ethnic identity and may choose to identify with an ethnic group by learning a language and adopting customs and beliefs.

Sometimes a person may feel part of a particular community but may still have trouble being completely accepted. Josiah Wilson was born in Haiti. When he was five months old, he was adopted by a Canadian First Nations doctor. Josiah grew up in Bella Bella, a small community in Western Canada. Because he was adopted into a Heiltsuk First Nation family, he is considered to be a status Indian (according to Canada's *Indian Act*). The Heiltsuk First Nation considers Josiah to be a nation member. Josiah loves to play basketball, but he was not allowed to play in an all-Native basketball tournament because none of

Love This!

PHOTOGRAPHERLONDON/DREAMSTIME.COM

According to the 2008 American *census*, about 15 percent of all new marriages in the United States each year are between people of different races. The website wearethe15percent.com has collected hundreds of photographs of mixed-race couples and families as a way of recognizing and celebrating the changing composition of American families.

his family members are blood relatives. According to tournament rules, players needed at least one-eighth North American Indigenous blood. After the family filed a complaint with the British Columbia Human Rights Tribunal, tournament organizers reconsidered their position. Now player eligibility is determined by providing legal documentation of First Nations membership and not by blood ancestry.

Josiah Wilson is not the only adopted child who has struggled to balance the reality of being born in one culture and raised in another. It's not always easy to completely fit into an adopted community, particularly when you don't look like most of the people around you. Some children long to connect with the language and traditions of their birth families. Adoptive parents may connect with families from the child's birthplace, provide language lessons or even travel back to the child's birth

Adopted children may look quite different from their parents or siblings.

FRENK AND DANIELLE KAUFMANN /DREAMSTIME.COM

I Believe in Love

When I was twelve or thirteen, there was a group of "cool" girls at my school. These girls wore makeup, their hair was always glossy, and they wore trendy clothes. I pretended I smoked (I had never smoked anything in my life), made up a boyfriend who lived in another town, and used lots of swear words whenever I was around them. When I was finally invited to sit with the cool girls at lunch, I was so disappointed. All they talked about was boys, makeup and hair. Quite often they said mean things about kids who were not part of their group. I didn't have much to contribute, and it wasn't long before I moved on and made some new friends who liked doing the same things I did. I never worried about joining the "cool" crowd again.

I met lots of people who shared my interests when I became involved with community theater as a teenager.

HELGA WILLIAMS

country to help the child better understand where they come from. Being raised in a completely different culture, though, can make it difficult for a person to ever feel they truly belong to the place where they were born. This can lead to feelings of loss and not quite fitting into the place where they grow up.

People from all backgrounds take part in Gay Pride celebrations.
TONY SPRACKETT

LGBTQ COMMUNITY

People use the phrase "LGBTQ community" all the time, but there is no one place where lesbian, gay, bisexual, transgender and queer people meet. Even so, the LGBTQ community is represented in most places in the world. In countries where *homosexuality* is illegal, members of the LGBTQ community may meet quietly in small groups to support each other and work on finding ways to slowly change local attitudes, beliefs and laws. In other places where people who identify as LGBTQ are well established and accepted, the community may host huge parades and celebrations during annual Pride festivals, embrace gay marriage and publicly battle against bullying or discrimination based on sexual orientation.

Let's Work Together

BIGANDT/DREAMSTIME.COM

In the Middle East, the conflict between Palestine and Israel has been going on for decades. The Peres Center for Peace in Israel runs a program that brings together Palestinian and Israeli children so they can play soccer. About 1,500 children take part in the program each year. Not only do the children play together on teams made up of players from both Palestine and Israel, but they also learn conflict-resolution skills and how to speak a little of the other group's language. By breaking down the barriers between the two groups of children, it's hoped that change will come to a region where distrust, fear and hatred have been all too common for far too long.

The rainbow flag has come to symbolize the diversity of the LGBTQ community. Each color also has a special meaning: red (life), orange (healing), yellow (sunlight), green (nature), blue (harmony/peace) and purple (spirit). TONY SPRACKETT

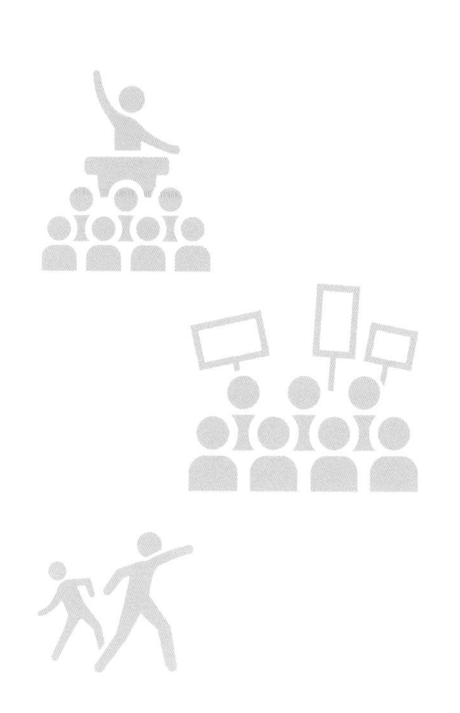

WHEN TENSIONS RISE BETWEEN GROUPS

Race, ethnicity and religion can result in strong bonds for members within a particular group. But sometimes terrible conflict arises when members of one group believe members of another are a threat.

Stereotypes are behaviors or traits that are said to belong to all the members of a group. Some stereotypes (like the idea that all Canadians are super polite) are harmless and nobody takes them too seriously. But when people believe wildly inaccurate and negative stereotypes, these beliefs can lead to conflict—and even war—between groups of people.

In the United States, tension between Caucasian Americans and African Americans has led to incidents of terrible violence.

In 1957, nine African American students enrolled in the previously all-white Little Rock High School. President Dwight D. Eisenhower ordered soldiers to protect the students as they arrived at school. US ARMY/WIKIPEDIA.ORG

One of the worst periods in recent American history was during the Civil Rights Movement in the 1950s and '60s. People of all races demanded that all citizens be treated equally. Others wanted to keep the old system of keeping racial groups apart through segregation. The battle left communities divided and resulted in horrific acts of violence as angry people defended their positions.

When my parents travelled in the state of Georgia in the southern United States during the 1960s, they were appalled to discover there were separate drinking fountains and bathrooms for people of color. Even in the movie theaters, certain seats were reserved for non-white patrons. Fortunately, official segregation is no longer the case in the United States, but race-based discrimination is still a sad reality worldwide.

Ethnic differences have been at the root of a number of devastating wars that have resulted in the deaths of men, women and children. The *civil war* in Rwanda in 1994 between two ethnic groups, the Hutus and Tutsis, left between 500,000 and one million people dead. Many more fled as refugees.

In the region formerly known as the country of Yugoslavia, civil war raged between 1991 and 2001. Multiple ethnic groups fought to determine who would control which areas. In the end, more than 130,000 people died and many more were injured. Others were forced to leave and begin new lives in other countries. Today the region is reasonably stable, and visitors can travel to half a dozen independent states, including Montenegro, Serbia and Croatia.

I LOVE MY COUNTRY

It's not uncommon for people to move from place to place. These moves could be to a new house in the same town or perhaps to a town or city not too far away. Sometimes, though, a move may take a person or family to a new country on the other side of the world.

In many places in the United States in 1938, it was normal to have separate drinking fountains for African Americans.

JOHN VACHON /WIKIPEDIA.ORG

COMMUNITY FACT:
The United Nations estimated there were more than 65 million refugees in the world at the end of 2015.

Mother and son refugees from Syria on the border between Serbia and Croatia.

NENAD MIHAJLOVIC/DREAMSTIME.COM

More than twelve million immigrants arrived at Ellis Island in Upper New York Bay between 1892 and 1954.
LEWIS HINE/WIKIPEDIA.ORG

Immigrants who settle in a new country may bring language, food and traditions with them. New immigrants seek out others who have come from the same place. For example, immigrants from China settled together in one area and created new communities known as Chinatowns in cities like San Francisco, New York and Vancouver. Shops, restaurants, schools and businesses serving these communities are often run by immigrants. Over many decades, Jewish immigrants have settled in certain neighborhoods in Montreal. Smoked meat sandwiches and unique bagels are a couple of tasty foods introduced by Jewish residents that are now widely enjoyed by locals and visitors alike.

After resettling in a new country, immigrants begin to learn the customs and language of their new home. How long does it take to begin to feel like you really belong in your new country? That depends.

My brother, who was born in Australia and grew up in Canada, has not lived in Canada for thirty years. He has a business in Tokyo, Japan, and lives part-time in Hawaii but still feels more Canadian than anything else.

Lion dancers are always popular at Chinese New Year parades held in Chinatowns all over the world.
ALUXUM/ISTOCK.COM

WHO'S IN AND WHO'S OUT?

You may think it would be easy to decide if someone is a member of a particular community or not. But often the question of membership is complicated. What happens when someone who has grown up in the deaf community using sign language receives a cochlear implant (a medical device that can help some deaf people hear) and is technically no longer deaf? Does this person still belong to the community of the deaf?

What about someone who adopts a new religion or moves to another country? At what point can that person truly feel part of their new community? What about someone who identifies with several different groups, perhaps at different times of their lives? When my mother first left her birth country of Germany and moved to England, she felt like an immigrant living in a foreign country. Years later, after moving to Canada, she rarely acknowledged her German background. Instead, when asked, she proudly told people, "I am Canadian." What about a cancer patient who, for a while, is a member of a tight-knit group at the local cancer institute but who then goes into remission? Is it odd to take part in hospital activities with friends who are still ill? After adults get divorced, do they also divorce the extended family of their former spouse?

In fact, it is possible to move between communities, to belong to more than one group at a time and to find common bonds with many different kinds of people at different points in time. What is always important is to be respectful and sensitive about other community members and how they feel about belonging to a particular group. It's just as important to consider how a former group member may feel about being left out when circumstances change. Losing a place on a sports team, for example, may be very difficult for a player who is injured or who does not do well in team tryouts.

COMMUNITY FACT:
According to the United Nations, in 2005 almost 200 million people emigrated from one country to another.

Let's Work Together

FABIO LACENTRA

Bookstores are places where communities of readers and writers gather to share their passion for books. In Paris, France, Shakespeare and Company, one of the world's most famous bookstores, has been welcoming writers since 1951, when it was established by George Whitman. This funny old shop with narrow staircases and many small rooms does more than just host an occasional poetry reading. Writers traveling through Paris are welcome to spend a few nights (or a few months) sleeping on simple beds tucked between the bookshelves! It's estimated that 30,000 writers have stayed here and become, for at least a short time, part of the literary community in Paris. The price? The deal is a writer must read at least one book each day, help out a bit in the store and write a one-page biography before leaving.

CHAPTER FOUR

Around the Globe

The flags of 193 member countries fly outside the United Nations headquarters in New York City.
ANDYKAZIE/SHUTTERSTOCK.COM

It can be a challenge to bring people in the same neighborhood together to work on a project. Imagine how hard it is to try to coordinate people from all over the world. The organizations and initiatives in this chapter all look at the big picture and try to bring people together to work on global projects.

UNITED NATIONS: BRINGING THE WORLD TOGETHER

World Wars I and II were major conflicts that involved dozens of nations around the globe. Millions of people were killed, injured or displaced during those wars. After the end of World War II, representatives from fifty countries met to create an international organization now known as the United Nations (UN).

In 2016, the UN estimated that almost five million refugees had fled from Syria since civil war broke out in their country. These Syrian children are in a refugee camp in Mafraq, Jordan. EHAB OTHMAN/SHUTTERSTOCK.COM

The intent of the UN was written down in its *charter* (a document that sets out an organization's goals). At the heart of the charter is the desire to encourage and "develop friendly relations among nations based on respect for the principle of equal rights and self-determination of peoples, and to take other appropriate measures to strengthen universal peace." A peaceful, cooperative world that ensures all people have access to food, water, shelter, a clean environment, healthcare and education is a lofty goal to be sure, but the many branches and divisions of the UN continue to work steadily toward achieving better living conditions for everyone. This work has been going on since the middle of the last century, and many improvements have been made, but there is still much to be done. The UN is involved with many worthy initiatives all over the world, including projects relating to health, education and human rights.

COMMUNITY FACT:
October 24 is United Nations Day. Each year a concert and speeches celebrate the official founding of the United Nations. Other commemorative acts may include art exhibitions, film screenings or special events. In 2016, for example, certain famous landmarks around the world were lit up with blue lights to share a message of "peace, development and human rights."

INTERNATIONAL COMMITTEE OF THE RED CROSS

Red Cross workers in Gori, Georgia, distribute food and other supplies at a refugee camp.
KOJOKU /SHUTTERSTOCK.COM

After witnessing a terrible battle at Solferino in Italy in 1859, a Swiss businessman called Henry Dunant wrote a book about his experiences helping the wounded and dying soldiers. In that book he also suggested that volunteers should be organized to help care for wounded soldiers during battle. He felt that nations at war should provide protection for medical personnel who were caring for those injured on the battlefield.

These basic ideas were initially adopted by several nations (Britain, France, Italy, Japan and the United States). Today, the International Committee of the Red Cross (ICRC) continues to provide assistance to those injured in battle.

A similar group of organizations known as the International Federation of Red Cross and Red Crescent Societies (IFRC) uses

I Believe in Love

When my daughter, Dani, was much younger, we both volunteered at the Victoria International Development Education Association (VIDEA) gift shop. VIDEA is an organization that works to promote understanding between different cultures and raise awareness for global issues. The store raised funds by selling handicrafts produced in developing nations and helped support VIDEA's programs and projects. The store no longer exists, but VIDEA still runs an annual Fair Trade Fair that brings together all kinds of vendors who sell products from around the world. Fair trade items range from coffee to handicrafts. Farmers and artisans are paid a fair price for their work in an effort to end poverty and support local economies.

Beautiful woven baskets like these from Ghana are often sold at Fair Trade fairs.
KOJOKU /SHUTTERSTOCK.COM

volunteers to help victims of disasters (like earthquakes, hurricanes or tsunamis) and health emergencies (such as disease outbreaks). Both the IFRC and the ICRC are part of a broader movement known as the International Red Cross and Red Crescent Movement, which also includes national Red Cross Societies in many countries around the world.

GLOBAL COLLABORATION

Although much of human history has been marked by conflicts and wars, there are also examples of times when people from many nations have worked together on a complex project. The island continent of Antarctica is not owned by any one nation. Instead, in 1959 twelve countries signed a treaty that protected the southernmost continent in the world: it would only ever be used for peaceful purposes. Scientific observations are to be made available to others, and all research stations are to be open for inspection.

The Human Genome Project brought together scientists from around the world who collaborated to map the human *genetic code*. Another massive project involving international cooperation is the International Space Station (ISS). More than twenty nations have helped keep the ISS running smoothly since the first component was sent into orbit in 1998.

DO YOU UNDERSTAND ME?

If you have ever travelled to a country where people speak a language you don't understand, you know how hard it can be to communicate with local people. When it's hard to communicate, it's easy for misunderstandings to develop and for people to get frustrated.

Esperanto is a made-up language that was invented to try to get around this problem. Created by a Polish eye doctor named L.L. Zamenhof, Esperanto was meant to be a language that would be easy to learn and could be understood by people

Love This!

RIA NOVOSTI/WIKIPEDIA.ORG

In 1982, ten-year-old Samantha Smith became known around the world after she wrote a letter to the then leader of the Soviet Union, Yuri Andropov, asking what Mr. Andropov was doing to prevent a war using nuclear weapons. Mr. Andropov wrote back and assured her he wanted peace as much as she did and invited her to come to the Soviet Union, which she did. Samantha became a junior *good-will ambassador*. She also visited Japan to participate in an international peace conference. Samantha wrote a book called *Journey to the Soviet Union*. Though Samantha died in a plane crash when she was just thirteen, the work she did to promote peace and understanding between two nations poised to go to war is still remembered today.

Love This!

NEEGZISTUOJA/WIKIPEDIA.ORG

Xiuhtezcatl (Shoe-Tez-Caht) Martinez has spoken out to raise awareness about climate change since he was very young. At the age of six he gave a speech at the Rio+20 United Nations Summit in Rio de Janeiro, Brazil, in 2012. At nine, Xiuhtezcatl began to perform as a hip-hop artist, and many of his songs have a strong environmental message. He is very active with Earth Guardians, an organization made up of musicians, artists and young activists. His desire to forge strong bonds with young people around the world and to raise awareness about environmental issues is rooted in his desire to protect our earth, air and water for future generations. Xiuhtezcatl may be young, but he proves that with a strong, clear voice and a message you believe in, you can make a huge difference in the world.

around the world. Esperanto (which means "one who hopes") is spoken by about two million people, making it the most popular made-up language in the world. By comparison, perhaps thirty people are fluent in Klingon, the made-up language spoken by Klingon aliens in the *Star Trek* universe.

Though Esperanto seems like a noble idea, many more people around the world speak English (it's estimated that 1.5 billion people speak English, though only about 375 million claim English as their first language). Many more people (about 900 million) speak Mandarin Chinese as their first language. Spanish, Arabic and Hindi round out the top five languages spoken in the world, all outnumbering Esperanto by a long shot. Nevertheless, there is something to be said for a language that began as an idealistic effort to bring the people of the world together.

FINDING A COMMON CAUSE

My mother used to say that if you want to bring people together, threaten them all with an invasion from Mars. Mom wasn't really worried about aliens taking over our planet, but she did understand something about human nature. People around the world come together every day to try to clean up the environment or protest against nuclear weapons or work as peace activists, all of which are issues important to everyone.

LONG-DISTANCE PARTNERSHIPS

A number of years ago I heard Canadian author Deborah Ellis speak about her work with women and children in Afghanistan who wanted to be able to go to school and learn to read and write. Deb donates the royalties from her popular novels *The Breadwinner* and *Parvana's Journey* to an organization called Canadian Women for Women in Afghanistan (CW4WAfghan). Funds raised go toward initiatives that provide access to

Organizations such as Canadian Women for Women in Afghanistan and the Malala Fund are dedicated to making sure girls all over the world have access to a good education. COURTESY OF CANADIAN WOMEN FOR WOMEN IN AFGHANISTAN

Let's Work Together

The group Little Women for Little Women in Afghanistan was founded in British Columbia in 2006 by nine-year-old Alaina Podmorow after she heard about the plight of girls in Afghanistan who really wanted to go to school but weren't able to do so. Since the group was formed it has raised over half a million dollars, which it has contributed to CW4WAfghan. Partnerships like this between groups of individuals in one country can make a huge difference in the lives of individuals on the other side of the globe.

In Tanzania, solar energy is an environmentally-friendly alternative to the electrical grid, bringing together entire commmunities. MOBISOL/WWW.PLUGINTHEWORLD.COM

education for girls and women in Afghanistan and create small community libraries in places where books are hard to come by.

Another example of people from far away coming to the aid of strangers can be seen after a terrible disaster. After a massive tsunami in the Indian Ocean in 2004 devastated hundreds of thousands of people's lives, help poured in from all over the world. Countries from Australia to Zimbabwe contributed more than $10 billion US to help the countries devastated by this natural disaster.

COMMUNITY FACT:
In the summer, as many as five thousand people from many different countries live in Antarctica. During the winter months, this number declines to fewer than one thousand. There are no Indigenous people in Antarctica.

In rural Tanzania, it's estimated that nine out of ten people do not have access to electricity at home. In 2013 the US government launched a project called Power Africa. Women in remote areas are trained to maintain solar power grids in their villages. With electricity, children are able to study after dark, and medicine and food can be refrigerated. Light frightens away predators, which helps protect a community's livestock. In villages where the grids are up and running, it's now possible to charge cell phones and computers without first making a long trek to a nearby town to pay for recharging services. In partnership with more than a hundred private companies, Power Africa is working hard to bring electricity to many more villages in sub-Saharan Africa.

BEYOND OURSELVES

Though most of this book has talked about the ways in which people come together to help each other, humans are also part of the broader ecosystem. We must learn to work with and care for our environment and the plants and creatures who share our planet.

Humans are not the only creatures on Earth who live and work together, forming strong communities. Ant colonies are complex communities. Individual ants have different jobs. Some defend the colony, others collect food, while others work in the nursery and feed and care for larvae. An ant city is organized a bit like a human city with different areas for food storage, raising larvae and getting rid of waste. A complex system of tunnels connects different areas in the same way roads connect different parts of a city.

Honey bees and bumble bees also live in complex communities and share responsibility for food gathering, raising young and defending the nest. Wolves hunt together to capture prey much larger than one wolf could manage to kill by itself. Whales and dolphins live in groups and communicate using sound. It's thought that these marine mammals may use unique sounds to identify each other and to coordinate their hunting efforts.

Like humans, honey bees also live in complex communities. LEHRER /SHUTTERSTOCK.COM

CONCLUSION

For as long as people have been around they have lived and worked together. Though at times it seems as though conflict and tension are inevitable, the desire to be kind and help each other is powerful. Looking after each other and the planet we live on is the best way to make sure our shared future is bright and prosperous.

Masai women in Kenya prepare to dance. For as long as people have lived on Earth, we have found ways to dance, sing, play and celebrate together. ZNM/DREAMSTIME.COM

Resources

Print

Ancona, George. *Can We Help? Kids Volunteering to Help Their Communities.* Sommerville, MA: Candlewick Press, 2015.

Bensen, Nigel C. *Psychology: A Graphic Guide.* London: Icon Books, 2007.

Jones, Kari. *A Fair Deal.* Victoria, BC: Orca Book Publishers, 2017.

Rappaport, Doreen. *Nobody Gonna Turn Me 'Round: Stories and Songs of the Civil Rights Movement.* Sommerville, MA: Candlewick Press, 2006.

Richardson, David. *Esperanto: Learning and Using the International Language.* CreateSpace Independent Publishing Platform, 2017.

Ruurs, Margriet. *Stepping Stones.* Victoria, BC: Orca Book Publishers, 2016.

Slavens, Elaine. *Peer Pressure: Deal With It Without Losing Your Cool.* Halifax: Formac Lorimer, 2004.

Stevenson, Robin. *Pride: Celebrating Diversity & Community.* Victoria, BC: Orca Book Publishers, 2016.

Online

4-H: http://4-h.org/about/global-network

ARC World Cruising Club: www.worldcruising.com/arc/event.aspx

British Tarantula Society: www.thebts.co.uk

Canadian Women for Women in Afghanistan: www.cw4wafghan.ca

CoAbode: www.coabode.org

Earth Guardians: www.earthguardians.org/xiuhtezcatl

Global Ecovillage Network: https://ecovillage.org

Hands Across the Sand: www.handsacrossthesand.com

International Committee of the Red Cross: www.icrc.org/en
Peres Center for Peace: www.peres-center.org
Tawang Monastery: http://tawangmonastery.org
UNICEF—Convention on Rights of the Child: www.unicef.org/crc
UNESCO: http://en.unesco.org
United Nations: www.un.org/en/index.html
VIDEA: http://videa.ca
The Villages Retirement Community: www.thevillages.com
Windsor House School: http://windsorhouseschool.org

Acknowledgments

When I was much younger, I went through a phase when I thought I would be happy and fulfilled living by myself on a very large, remote piece of land. How wrong I was! A lifetime of making connections with family, friends, neighbors, writers, farmers, sailors and climbers has shown me that our great strengths as humans are only fully realized when we cooperate with others. Far too many individuals and organizations have played a role in my perspective shift to possibly try to mention them all here. One group, though, deserves a special shout-out, and that's the team at Orca Book Publishers. Your dedication to bringing stories and information to young readers is an act of faith in future generations. Thank you all for creating such beautiful books on so many important topics and doing your best to get them into the hands of readers all over the world.

Glossary

adoption— a process whereby a person assumes the parenting of a child and all rights and responsibilities from the biological parent or parents

age cohort—a group of people of a similar age

birth parent—a biological parent as opposed to an adoptive parent

census—an official count or survey of a population, typically recording various details of individuals such as age, gender and ethnicity

charter—a document that sets out an organization's goals

commune—a group of people living together and sharing possessions and responsibilities, sometimes known as a collective or a cooperative

community—a group of people living in the same place or having a particular characteristic in common; also a feeling of fellowship with others as a result of sharing common attitudes, interests and goals

convent—a group of nuns; also the place where a group of nuns lives

cryptophasia—a phenomenon of a language developed by twins (identical or fraternal) that only the two children can understand

culture—the beliefs, customs, arts and way of life of a particular society, group, place or time

discrimination—the practice of unfairly treating a person or group of people differently from other people or groups of people, especially on the basis of race, age or gender

ecovillage—an intentional community that has a strong focus on environmental and economic sustainability

Esperanto—a made-up language that was invented to be easy to learn and could be understood by people around the world

ethnicity—the state of belonging to a social group that has a common national or cultural tradition

extended family—a family that extends beyond the nuclear family, including grandparents, aunts, uncles and other relatives

fair trade—international trade based on dialogue, transparency and respect in which fair prices are paid to producers in developing countries

foster parents—people who provide short-term care for children who can't live with their parents for some reason

genetic code—the set of rules by which information encoded in genetic material (DNA or RNA sequences) is translated into proteins (amino acid sequences) by living cells

goodwill ambassador—a person who advocates for a specific cause on the basis of its notability, by delivering goodwill or promoting ideals from one entity to another

homosexuality—sexual attraction to people of one's own sex

immigrant—a person who comes to a country to take up permanent residence

intentional community—a planned residential community designed to have a high degree of social cohesion and teamwork

isolation—to be or remain alone or apart from others

leprosy (Hansen's disease)—a contagious bacterial disease that affects the skin, mucous membranes and nerves, causing discoloration and lumps on the skin and, in severe cases, disfigurement and deformities

Maslow's Hierarchy of Needs—a theory proposed by Abraham Maslow in 1943 that describes five types of needs that motivate human behavior

misogyny—a dislike of, contempt for or ingrained prejudice against women

monastery—a group of monks; also the place where a group of monks lives

nuclear family—a family group that consists only of father, mother and children

ostracize—to exclude someone from a society or group

overpopulation—the condition of having a population that exceeds the environment's ability to sustain that population

persecute—to oppress, abuse or mistreat someone, especially because of race or political and religious beliefs

quarantine—the isolation of people, animals or things (such as plants) out of a certain area to prevent the spread of disease or pests

racism—prejudice or discrimination against someone of a different race based on the belief that one's own race is superior

refugee—a person who has been forced to leave their country in order to escape war, persecution or natural disaster

same-sex couple—two people of the same gender who are in a relationship

segregation—the enforced separation of different racial groups in a country, community or establishment

stereotype—a behavior or trait that is attributed to all members of a group

Index

Page numbers in **bold** *indicate an image; there may also be text related to the same topic on that page*

Index (continued)